Commercial Due Diligence in Private Equity

-

A checklist for investors

HENRY LEON BLACKMANN

DEDICATION

Dedicated to all individuals who are working hard to become the better version of themselves. The sky is the limit.

CONTENTS

FOREWORD

This book may be useful for anyone interested in private equity. For people new to the industry, this book may be a good introduction into commercial due diligence from the perspective of a private equity investor. By reading and studying this book, one will get a good understanding of how private equity investors think about companies they potentially invest in and what characteristics those companies should have in order to be seen as an attractive company from a commercial point of view. For experienced investors, this book can act as a checklist to make sure one considers all relevant commercial aspects when conducting due diligence. Given the broad range of different investment strategies and transaction types in the private equity industry, this book does not claim to be applicable in every private equity transaction. Neither does this book claim to provide an instruction to generate attractive returns nor does it represent any kind of investment advice. It is also important to bear in mind that this book mainly refers to leveraged buyout when talking about private equity transactions. To a certain extent, the discussed aspects may also hold for venture capital transactions or any other kind of private markets transaction. However, certain aspects discussed in this book may be less relevant or not relevant at all in the context of such transactions.

This book does not provide any kind of investment advice. All comments and statements solely reflect the author's opinion.

1 INTRODUCTION

Private equity investors buy companies, professionalize them over the course of three to five years and then sell them for a higher price than they have initially paid, thereby making a return. When deciding on whether to buy a company or not, private equity investors do due diligence on the company they want to buy. They do so to analyze how attractive the company is as an investment. Those companies usually need to be analyzed from different points of views, i.e. there are different kinds of due diligence work that need to be done. The most important areas of due diligence can be categorized as follows:

- **Commercial Due Diligence:** Analyzing the business model of the company and the market it operates in
- **Financial Due Diligence:** Analyzing the balance sheet, the profit and loss statement as well as the cash flow statement. In addition, the financial due diligence includes the structuring of the transaction
- **Technology and IT due diligence:** Analyzing technologies that are key to the success of the company as well as analyzing the overall IT setup of the company. This area of due diligence gains more significance as most parts of our economy become digital.
- **Legal and Regulatory Due Diligence:** Analyzing the legal and regulatory environment of the company, its customer/supplier contracts as well as the contracts regarding the transaction itself

- **Tax Due Diligence:** Analyzing the tax situation of the company to seize the future tax burden of the company
- **Environmental, Social and Governance (ESG) Due Diligence:** Analyzing the ESG efforts of the company as well as the ESG risks of the company

It is important to bear in mind that all areas of due diligence are important in order to make a final investment decision. However, in a private equity context, commercial due diligence may arguably be the most important area of due diligence as you invest into an entrepreneurial activity whose aim is to generate positive earnings. If the business model of your company is not strong enough, you won't be able to generate revenues and, in the end won't be able to generate positive earnings. Merely a superior technology (Technology Due Diligence) or great ESG efforts of a company (ESG due diligence) won't generate any earnings. However, positive earnings are the basis to generate returns for investors as the following chapter will elaborate on.

2 VALUE CREATION AND RETURN GENERATION IN PRIVATE EQUITY

There are three ways to create value and to generate returns in private equity. First, by increasing earnings, especially operating earnings. Private equity investors mostly look at earnings before interest, tax, depreciation and amortization (EBITDA) as the preferred operating return metric. In order to increase EBITDA, the company either needs to increase revenues (top line effect) or increase the EBITDA margin (bottom line effect). Ideally, private equity investors manage to do both, i.e. to sell more units of a given product or service and increase the earnings margin of those products or services. Second, private equity investors can generate a return by simply selling the same company for a higher valuation, i.e. for higher earnings multiples (usually measured as Enterprise value (EV) to EBITDA) compared to the earnings multiples they paid (this is called "multiple arbitrage"). Third, assuming the company was bought partly by using debt financing, private equity investors generate a return by using the firm's cash flow to repay the debt over the course of the holding period. All else equal, less net debt means a higher value of the investor's equity value as the enterprise value is the sum of the equity value and the net debt value.

The following example shall illustrate the framework of generating returns in private equity. Some may call this the value creation framework in private equity, whereas "creating value" means nothing else but increasing the equity value of a company.

3

Private equity investors usually buy into the equity of a company. Therefore, the investor makes a return in case the equity value of the company increases.

	at investment	at exit	Value Creation	
Revenues (USD Mio.)	100	150	96	Top line effect
EBITDA-Margin (%)	12%	16%	48	Bottom line effect
EBITDA (USD Mio.)	12	24	144	Value creation through EBITDA increase
EV/EBITDA Multiple (x)	10	12	24	Value creation through multiple arbitrage
Enterprise Value (USD Mio.)	120	288		
Net Debt (USD Mio.)	50	10	40	Value Creation through debt repayment
Equity Value (USD Mio.)	**70**	**278**	**208**	**Total Value creation**
			4.0x	**Return for equity investor**

In the example above the private equity investor buys a company that generates USD 100 Mio. in revenues per year. The EBITDA margin is 12%, i.e. the company generates USD 12 Mio. in EBITDA per year. The private equity investor bought the company for an enterprise value (EV) to EBITDA multiple of ten times, valuing the company at an enterprise value of USD 120 Mio. The private equity investor financed the enterprise value with USD 70 Mio. of his own equity capital and the remaining USD 50 Mio. were financed with debt from a bank. During the holding period, the private equity investor managed to increase revenues by 50% from USD 100 Mio. to USD 150 Mio. while simultaneously increasing the EBITDA margin from 12% to 16%. This created USD 144 Mio. in equity value for the private equity investor whereas USD 96 Mio. was due to the fact that he managed to increase revenues (top line effect) and USD 48 Mio. due to the fact that he managed to increase the EBITDA margin (bottom line effect). Both effects increased the EBITDA of the company from USD 12 Mio. to USD 24 Mio.

The investor bought the company for a valuation of ten times the EBITDA, which translates into an enterprise value of USD 120 Mio. (USD 12 Mio. multiplied by ten). After the holding period, he is able to sell the company for twelve times EBITDA, i.e. the valuation level increased by two turns of EBITDA (multiple arbitrage). Even if EBITDA would have been flat throughout the whole holding period, the investor would have generated USD 24 Mio. [(12x-10x) multiplied by USD 12 Mio. EBITDA] in value simply through selling for a higher EV/EBITDA multiple than the investor paid initially.

Finally, the investor created value by using the company's cash flow to repay the debt, such that the net debt value decreased from USD 50 Mio. to USD 10 Mio. during the holding period. The value created equals the difference between the net debt value at the beginning and the net debt value at the exit (USD 50 Mio – USD 10 Mio. = USD 40 Mio.), because all else equal, by decreasing the net debt value, the equity value increases for any given enterprise value.

In sum, the investor created USD 208 USD Mio. in equity value, which equals a return of about four times his invested equity capital (USD 278 Mio. divided by USD 70 Mio.). Assuming a holding period of five years, this reflects an annual return of ca. 32% $[(278/70)^{(1/5)}-1]$.

This value creation illustration should act as the starting point for every discussion about commercial due diligence. Why? Because every aspect discussed during a commercial due diligence should be assessed on the basis of the question whether it will help to increase the equity value of the company. In the end, every investor wants to generate a positive return on its investment and the commercial due diligence is just one way of assessing the probability that a certain company will be able to increase its equity value for the investor. Therefore, every aspect that will be discussed in the following chapters should be related to the question of how that aspect will affect the value creation profile of a company.

3 REVENUE MODEL

(relates to top line effect)

3.1 Diversified portfolio of mission critical products and service portfolio

The company should have a broad range of products and services that can be offered to customers such that revenues do not depend on the success of one product or one service. In addition, **the product or service should be mission critical for the customer**, i.e. the customer really needs the offering as it adds a lot of value to him and there are no alternatives or substitutes for it.

3.2 Broad value chain coverage

Customers will appreciate it if a company has offers along the value chain. The customer will regard the company as **"one stop shop"** where they can shop and get everything they need. Think of a media company that offers music streaming to its clients, but at the same time also offers video streaming. By offering music streaming and video streaming at the same time, the client only needs to interact with one provider and does not need an additional provider for streaming videos besides streaming music. This enhances the company's revenue generation capabilities and saves the customer time as well as energy while increasing his satisfaction.

3.3 Revenue visibility

Ideally a company can offer a high degree of revenue visibility, i.e. revenues can be predicted with a high degree of certainty and lead to high recurring revenues. This can usually be achieved through subscription-based contracts or multi year contracts where the customer subscribes to a certain service or the customer enters into an agreement with the company to supply him for several years. Good examples of subscription-based business models are software as a service (SaaS) companies, where other businesses or individuals pay for using software. Given that those customers rely on certain software, you know that they will use it over and over again. Hence the revenue generated from those clients is highly predictable and recurring.

3.4 Flexible and optimized pricing policy

Investors should look for flexible pricing opportunities in order to fully **absorb clients purchasing power through cross selling or upselling**. For instance, a pricing policy should allow for product bundles which offer the customer a discount if he purchases not one product/service but two or more. In that way, a company fully absorbs the clients purchasing power while deepening the relationship with the customer. Think about an electronics manufacturer who sells computers to individuals. If someone purchases a computer, it is not unlikely that this individual is also thinking about purchasing a printer or a monitor. If a company offers an attractive bundle, the clients may purchase all three items and not just the computer, thereby increasing the wallet share per client which results in increased revenues for the company. In addition, an investor should always check whether price increases are possible given what competitors charge. Revenues can be easily increased, simply by increasing prices in case current prices are below market standards and in case customers will tolerate those price increases.

4 COST STRUCTURE
(relates to bottom line effect)

4.1 Fixed costs versus variable costs

Investors usually prefer variable costs over fixed costs. Fixed costs pose a certain risk as they cannot be eliminated immediately. This is dangerous in times of economic downturns or in case the company is underperforming. In such situations, revenues decline but costs stay relatively stable, resulting in declining earning margins. Variable costs only occur in case revenues are generated, hence do not possess the same risk to a company as fixed costs. Therefore, most investors will favor **low fixed costs**. Low fixed cost also helps when a company aims to expand into a new market (segments) as the upfront investments (for fixed costs) are relatively low.

4.2 Cost drivers and operational leverage

When analyzing the cost structure, investors prefer **controllable cost drivers** in order to be able to predict the future costs of the business. Costs that are not certain and not controllable, e.g. the price of a raw material like oil that are very volatile and hard to predict, pose a risk to the future earnings of the company and can ultimately jeopardize the whole investment case. Those cost drivers might be hedged through financial derivatives, but those hedges are usually expensive to implement, hence reducing earnings as well.

Examples of controllable cost drivers are office equipment or insurance payments since those costs can be predicted pretty accurately over the period of 3-5 years (which is the typical holding period of a private equity investor).

Besides controllable cost drivers, investors also look for **high operating leverage** in companies. Operating leverage refers to a company's ability to generate higher earnings margins the more products or services they sell. Thus, the next unit sold has a higher earnings margin than the previous unit sold, because the more units sold the more fixed cost can be spread across a large number of units sold, while variable cost may also go down e.g. due to higher price negotiation power towards your suppliers. Through this mechanism, operating leverage enables a company to expand profitably. Therefore, private equity investors favor companies with high operating leverage since it provides a way to increase earnings of a company simply through expanding a company's activities, e.g. opening additional stores in other states.

4.3 Working capital and capital expenditure (capex) requirements

Private equity investors usually look for companies that have **low working capital requirements** as well as low capex requirements. Working capital ties up capital in inventory and accounts receivable and prevents the capital to be productive, i.e. to generate a return. Therefore, a high working capital creates high opportunity costs because you could have used the tied-up capital to invest in other return generating assets or business activities. Alternatively, the tied-up cash could have been used to repay your debt, thereby reducing the debt value and increasing the equity value at the time of selling the company.

Similarly, private equity investors shy away from companies with high working capital requirements. Why? Because capex investments usually require a lot of cash, which then cannot be used to repay the debt of the company (value creation through debt repayment) or used for other return generating business activities like making tuck-in acquisitions (e.g. buying a smaller competitor). Hence, all things equal, private equity investors will always favor a company with **low capex requirements**.

4.4 Earning margins and cash flow conversion

Private equity investors usually look for companies with **high earnings margins and high cash flow conversion**. Earnings margins are the ratio of earnings (measured in EBITDA, EBIT or net income) to revenues. An earnings margin of 30% means that for every 100 USD in revenues, 30 USD remains in net profit after deducting all the costs. However, earnings do not necessarily equal cash flows. Therefore, private equity investors look also for a high cash flow conversion, i.e. earnings should ideally match with cash flows and not consist of non-cash items or be reduced by high capex investments that lower cash flows. Private equity investors are keen on high cash flows as those cash flows enable them to repay the debt (value creation through debt repayment). Hence, private equity investors appreciate companies where earnings do not contain a lot of non-cash items and where most of the earnings are converted to cash flows that flow into the company (high cash flow conversion). The cash flow conversion can be calculated by dividing the cash flow of a company by its earnings. The higher the percentage of this ratio the better for private equity investors as this means a high percentage of the annual earnings can be used to repay debt and thereby creating equity value.

5 ORGANIZATION

(relates to all value creation effects)

5.1 Geographical footprint

Geographical diversification is something that private equity investors are usually looking for. Investors especially analyze in which regions a company has its manufacturing facilities and offices. Having production facilities and offices in multiple different locations reduces the risks associated with a specific region and increases the flexibility of a company. Geopolitical conflicts, broken supply chains, travel restrictions and rising commodity shortages demand flexibility in terms of sourcing capabilities, production capabilities and selling capabilities. Especially with regard to the latter, private equity investors also analyze whether there are other regional markets that are currently not served by the company but could potentially be served given the company's production facilities and offices. Those untapped markets represent additional revenue sources and can boost future revenues (value creation through top line effect).

5.2 Intellectual properties and patents

Intellectual properties and patents can be a meaningful source of value creation potential. Especially patented technologies or approaches to produce a product to customers are of high value to private equity investors as this increases the competitive strength of the company compared to existing/new competitors. In addition, **intellectual properties and patents can be monetized** by making them available to other companies in exchange for a license fee. Companies may also sell their patents, which would be another way to monetize them in case the private equity investor does not deem the patents to be useful going forward.

5.3 Corporate structure and internal processes

Private equity investors usually analyze the corporate structure and internal processes of a company very carefully. A **lean corporate structure and efficient processes** can reduce costs significantly and thereby increase earnings (bottom line effect). However, this does not mean that private equity investors will buy only companies with lean corporate structures and efficient processes. It is rather the opposite. Private equity investors usually buy companies with complex corporate structures and inefficient processes because part of most private equity investors' value creation agenda is to eliminate those inefficiencies which in turn creates value through increased EBITDA.

5.4 Management tools and IT infrastructure

Efficient processes often include the use of **state-of-the-art IT tools and software for customer relationship management, enterprise resource planning as well as financial controlling**. Most companies that private equity investors buy do not possess those management tools or use outdated ones. However, it is crucial for a company to have a crystal-clear view on how much resources each process within the company consumes, what their relationship to their existing and potential customers looks like and what the overall financial health of the company looks like. Only good monitoring and management tools can achieve that. Most companies that private equity investors buy lack all of those tools and therefore fail to manage the company efficiently based on actual data rather than based on the gut feeling of the top management.

6 MARKET

(relates to top line effect)

6.1 Size of total addressable market

Private equity investors usually prefer business models that target a **large total addressable market (TAM)**. The larger the addressable market, the larger your revenue potential, i.e. the more money there is potentially to be made in this market (top line effect). Investors usually break the TAM further down into the **serviceable available market (SAM)** and the **serviceable obtainable market (SOM)**. The SAM is the part of the TAM that your business can potentially serve. For instance, if you are only operating in one part of your country, then the TAM is not reflecting your overall revenue potential, as you are only able to service a certain part of your country, which is only representing a fraction (i.e. the SAM) of the TAM. The SAM can further be broken down into the part of the market/segment of customers that you can realistically win and the part of the SAM that is unlikely to become your customer. Maybe some of your direct competitors have locked up their clients in 10+ year contracts. In that situation, those clients are part of the SAM, but it is highly unlikely that you will win them as customers since they have to stick to their existing contracts (because otherwise they have to pay significant fines if they cancel those contracts, which usually does not make sense for them). Hence, the SOM is the best approximation of the market that reflects your revenue potential. Be

13

aware that the SOM itself is not the only factor that determines your revenue potential. As will be discussed in the next chapter ("Competition"), the second important factor is the market share that you are able to gain in the SOM. Your revenue potential is higher if you can realistically acquire a market share of 40% in a market with a SOM of USD 100 Mio. (potential revenue of USD 40 Mio.) than your revenue potential when you can realistically acquire only 5% market share in a SOM of USD 500 Mio. (potential revenue of USD 25 Mio.).

6.2 Historical and future expected growth rates

Private equity investors usually look at the historic rates at which the market, in which the company is operating, has grown. They try to identify the drivers that led to this historic market growth and try to estimate the **future growth rate of the market**. For instance, if the market has grown strongly mainly because more and more people have purchased a smartphone for the first time, then the growth rates may decline in the future since most people already have a smartphone and only few smartphone buyers can be regarded as first-time purchasers of smartphones. In addition, other factors may arise that affect the market growth going forward, which haven't affected the market growth in the past (e.g. because customers' preferences have changed). Forecasting the future market growth can be a complicated and challenging task. Therefore, private equity investors usually interview industry experts to ask them about their view on future growth rates of the market and trends in the market in general. Why is the future growth of the market so important? - Because it provides a good starting point for estimating a company's future growth rate. If the market is expected to grow by 5% p.a., then a company that is operating in that market may grow in line with, above or below the market. If the company grows in line with the market, then the revenues of that company will likely grow by 5% p.a. as well. If the company grows above (below) the market, then the question an investor needs to answer is how much more (less) the company is growing compared to the overall market. In most cases, companies are growing a few percentage points above or below the overall market. It is unlikely that the market is growing at 5% while a company that is operating in that market is growing by 80%. In such a situation, investors should rethink whether they have defined the market correctly, in which the company is operating.

6.3 End-market exposure

While analyzing the market in which a company operates is very important, it is equally important to look at **the end-market which the company is exposed to**. For instance, a company that develops software for auto dealers is primarily operating in the software market. However, it is also affected by the development of the auto industry. If car sales are going down, the company may add fewer new subscribers to their software products as auto dealers are reluctant to invest and add new costs to their profit and loss statement. Therefore, private equity investors always look at what other industries affect the market that the company is operating in.

6.4 Cyclicality

Investors carefully look at how prone a company's financials (especially revenues and earnings) are to economic fluctuations during boom times (economic expansions) and even more important during bust times (economic recessions). A company with a more **cyclical business model (high correlation to economic fluctuations)** represents a riskier investment opportunity since the company's financials are harder to predict than for companies with **non-cyclical business models (low correlation to economic fluctuations)**. Therefore, investors usually tend to favor non-cyclical business models over highly cyclical business models. Healthcare, utilities and non-discretionary staples are examples for industries where one can find a lot of non-cyclical business models since those products/services are needed irrespective of the current economic situation. In contrast, construction, automotive, discretionary staples or semiconductors are industries that represent a lot of cyclical business models.

6.5 Regulatory environment and tariffs

Private equity investors usually shy away from heavily regulated industries such as healthcare, utilities, gambling or telecommunications. **Regulations may create significant hurdles and challenges to do business**. In addition, regulations also create additional risk as regulations may change, leading to unexpected effects on business models. However, some investors see those challenges/risks as opportunities. Because of the complex and risky nature of regulated industries, fewer investors consider investing in those industries, which results in lower competition. Investors that acquire industry specific knowledge and that know how to navigate those regulations may find attractive investment opportunities. Most often they invest in business models within regulated industries that have as little regulatory risk as possible, e.g. healthcare service companies. Those companies provide essential services to healthcare companies but aren't as affected by regulations as those healthcare companies they count as their clients. In addition, investors also analyze whether a company might be affected by other laws, regulations or legal conditions such as tariffs. Think about trade wars that come with high tariffs on certain foreign goods, which create significant supply chain hurdles resulting in increased input prices. This can turn formerly profitable business models into unprofitable business models, creating severe solvency problems for affected companies.

7 COMPETITION
(relates to all value creation effects)

7.1 Market Share and market competitiveness

Private equity investors pay close attention to the competitive landscape of a company. Market shares provide a good indication for this. Private equity investors like to buy **the number one or the number two player in a given industry**, i.e. the company with the largest or second largest market share. A large market share usually comes with large economies of scale, i.e. purchasing power (for input goods), price setting power (for selling the products), operating leverage (diminishing fixed and variable costs) and a strong reputation (given the company's omnipresence).

7.2 Market fragmentation/concentration

Related to the previous aspect regarding market shares, private equity investors like industries that are highly fragmented, i.e. **industries where there is no other dominant player** besides the company that they buy. A lot of smaller competitors with small market shares provide ample opportunities for strategic add-on acquisitions. Such transactions enable inorganic growth, whereas sales can be grown and cost synergies can be drawn, thereby increasing the overall profitability.

7.3 Barriers to entry

Private equity investors, like any other equity investor, prefer to invest in **business models and industries with high barriers of entry**. High barriers of entry decrease competition from new entrants. Barriers of entry can be due to technological reasons (very complicated tech needed), due to legal reasons (e.g. licenses needed to be active in industry), due to financial reasons (Capital-intensive business model that require large initial start-up investments) or due to reputational reasons (customers prefer well-known brands over new unknown brands). Those business models and industries are less prone to competition and disruption from new entrants like business models with low barriers to entry. The commercial airline industry is an example of an industry with low barriers to entry. Not much is needed to enter this industry except the capital to lease some airplanes, some human resources (pilots, flight attendance etc.) and starting/landing slots at airports. That's why there are always popping up new airlines which, in tough economic times, may disappear as fast as they have appeared in the beginning.

7.4 Strategic positioning

Investors carefully assess the **strategic position of a company's products/services**. E.g. whether a company offers a low-cost product for the mass market (high sales volume but low margins due to high competition/low barriers of entry) or whether a company offers a highly customized high-quality premium product (low sales volume as there are fewer potential customers but higher margins due to lower competition/higher barriers to entry). It cannot be said whether private equity owners favor a certain strategic positioning over the other. But private equity investors will certainly analyze the strategic positioning carefully since it affects almost every other aspect discussed in this book (e.g. pricing power towards supplier/customers, revenue model, cost structures, competition, growth potential etc.)

7.5 Differentiation and unique selling proposition (USP) compared to direct competitors

When analyzing the products and services of a company, private equity investors assess the **unique selling proposition (USP) and differentiation factor of the product/service**. They basically ask what kind of value the product/service brings to its clients and how does this value differ when comparing it to the value provided by other competing products/services. Ideally you want a product whose value is unique and of very high importance to your clients.

8 CUSTOMERS

(relates to top line effect)

8.1 Customer diversification

Private equity investors like companies that have a **well-diversified customer base** as this reduces the risks of revenue declines when losing customers. Investors usually look at the percentage of overall revenues that the Top 5 or Top 10 customers stand for. Private equity investors also try to increase customer diversification during their ownership, as this increases revenue visibility, thereby reducing the overall risk of the investment. Future sellers will also pay a premium for companies with well diversified customer bases over companies with concentrated customer bases.

8.2 Customer history and customer churn

When analyzing the customer base of a company, private equity investors also look at the customer history, i.e. the **duration (or lifetime) of each customer relationship**. Obviously, investors favor loyal clients, who have been clients for many years as this decreases the likelihood of clients switching to other competitors. Investors will also carefully check if and why customers left the company to work with other competitors (customer churn). High historic customer churn is usually a warning signal for investors and the reasons behind it need to be understood well in order to assess the customer churn risk going forward.

8.3 Customer pipeline

Besides a company's customer history, private equity investors also carefully assess the customer pipeline, i.e. **the pipeline of potentially new customers** that the company is currently trying to win as customers. The pipeline is important as this gives investors guidance towards the extent of new customers the company is most likely to win over the coming years, which ultimately affects a company's ability to increase revenues. The customer pipeline is obviously highly correlated to the performance of a company's sales team. All things equal, the larger your sales team, the more potential customers a company can talk to and the more likely a company will acquire new customers.

8.4 Customer's price sensitivity

Private equity investors carefully assess to what extent a company can increase prices for its products and services. This partly depends on the price sensitivity of customers. If the price sensitivity of customers is low, they won't switch to other providers or substitute your product with another product when a company increases its prices. In such a situation, investors will also label this situation as companies having a strong pricing power, i.e. **they can increase prices without any negative consequences**.

8.5 Customer solvency

Investors look carefully at customers' solvency, especially at **the solvency of the company's largest customers**. Investors will shy away from companies whose customers have a weak financial profile as this increases the likelihood that the company won't get paid by its customers. Therefore, investors favor companies with blue chip companies (large well-known companies) as their customers. The likelihood of those blue-chip companies becoming insolvent is significantly lower than for smaller companies.

8.6 Customer satisfaction and feedback

Private equity investors usually talk to the customers of a company before they invest in the company. They do so to get feedback from the customer on the things they like about the company (e.g. high quality of product) and the things they do not like about the company (e.g. poor customer services). Investors do these **customer reference calls** to assess the overall customer satisfaction and to identify areas of improvement. Overall low customer satisfaction may also indicate a high likelihood of losing customers in the near future (customer churn).

8.7 Customer trends

Talking to the customers of a company may also reveal **changes in the customer's preference** going forward. Maybe customers will value certain aspects (e.g. fast and free customer service) higher than they did in the past. Those preferences may change as their business models change due to trends in their respective industries. Investors need to be aware of those trends as every company needs to respond to their clients' needs and preferences. Usually, companies who can adapt to their clients' needs will win significant business from other competitors.

9 SUPPLIERS

(relates to bottom line effect)

9.1 Supply chain complexity

The Covid-19 pandemic highlighted the **risks that are embedded in complex supply chains**. Therefore, private equity investors assess a company's supply chain carefully, to identify any risk that could potentially affect the business activities negatively. Risk could be that for certain inputs a company has only one supplier. If that supplier cannot deliver those inputs, the whole manufacturing process stops. Or the only supplier for an input is located in a country that is well known for powerful worker unions and frequent labor strikes. Hence, robust and reliable supply chains are a positive aspect for any company.

9.2 Supplier portfolio

Like with customers, private equity investors also analyze a company's list of suppliers. Ideally, that **list of suppliers is long and well diversified in terms of size and geography**. Investors will favor a well-diversified list of suppliers, where every supplier can be replaced by another supplier on the list, irrespective the volume of goods (i.e. no supplier should be too small such that they cannot deliver the needed amount of inputs). Investors will also favor a list of suppliers that are well diversified in terms of geography, such that if one geographical region faces problems that hinders exports (e.g. tariffs, export bans, lock downs etc.), another supplier from another geographical region can replace those supplies.

9.3 Supplier pricing power

Like with customers, private equity investors assess the **pricing power of suppliers**. The pricing power usually depends on how diversified a company's list of suppliers is. If there are multiple alternative suppliers that can easily replace another supplier, the pricing power of suppliers is probably low. Pricing power of suppliers is important as this may severely affect your cost structure in case you cannot avoid price increases of your input goods by switching to another supplier.

9.4 Supplier reliability

Reliability of your suppliers is key in order to guarantee smooth processes within the company. This is especially important for time-sensitive production processes that are based on "just in time" supply chains. The reliability of suppliers can be assessed by analyzing the historic track record of suppliers. If a supplier never missed any deadline and always delivered the pre-defined amount of goods on time, chances are high he will do so in the future. In addition, investors can assess the reliability by screening the suppliers manufacturing capabilities (amount of production sites, number of employees etc.) and by conducting reference calls with other customers of the respective suppliers.

10 MANAGEMENT AND OTHER HUMAN RESOURCES

(relates to all value creation effects)

10.1 Quantity and quality of full-time employees

Employees can be mission-critical success factors for companies. Therefore, investors carefully assess the **quantity and the quality of a company's full-time employees (FTE)**. Assessing the quantity of FTE is important to make sure the company has enough human resources to execute the business model successfully. Investors will often realize that a company may lack human resources in a certain department (e.g. too few sales people in order to grow significantly) or that a company has too many FTEs in a certain department (e.g. too many administrative people that perform non-mission critical tasks).

Investors also carefully assess the quality (i.e. the skills, capabilities and know-how) of a company's FTEs. Of special focus are any skills or any know-how that is highly success-relevant (e.g. scientists within a pharma company that have expert knowledge regarding the development and manufacturing of certain drugs) as well as the top management. The top management usually includes the chief executive officer (CEO), chief financial officer (CFO), chief operating officer (COO), chief technology officer (CTO) and others. Those roles are crucial for any company and especially for private equity backed companies. The top management is in charge of successfully executing the strategy. Therefore, private equity managers spend a lot of time and effort to make sure companies have the best top management they possibly can find for this company. The first question usually is whether the current top management meets the quality requirements of a private equity manager. Ideally, they meet the quality requirements and the private equity manager can build on the top management's knowledge regarding the company and its processes. More often than not, the top management's quality is not good enough such that private equity managers have to replace the current top management with the right people. Private equity managers usually work with headhunters to identify the right candidates for the CEO, CFO, COO etc. position. Often, they hire top management people from a company's direct competitors.

10.2 Founder/Seller rollover

When private equity investors buy a company from the founder or another private individual, they usually **offer the seller to rollover the proceeds of the sale into the company**. They do so, to make sure the seller stays involved in the company such that the know-how and network of the seller does not get lost. It also signals continuity to the current employees, customers, suppliers and any other stakeholders. From a financial point of view, rolling over some proceeds into the company makes a lot of sense for the seller. They usually can generate a very attractive return on their rollover in case the private equity transaction is successful. Founder/seller rollovers are very common for buyout strategies that aim at being the first institutional investor in a company.

10.3 Existence and strength of labor unions

Depending on the geography and the industry, labor unions may exist at certain companies. Those unions could make it difficult for private equity investors to implement their value creation strategy, especially if unions prevent cost cuts and closures of manufacturing sites. Restructuring programs are hard to implement if unions oppose them. Therefore, **private equity investors usually shy away from companies where there are strong labor unions**.

10.4 Sales and marketing resources

Most founder-owned companies have developed great products and technologies over the years, but they often do a poor job in selling their products. Therefore, private equity investors carefully assess the sales and marketing approach of a company before they invest. Private equity investors can create a lot of value by installing professional sales and marketing processes as well as hiring additional sales and marketing professionals to acquire new clients and increase revenues. Therefore, sales and marketing professionals are usually among the key hires (besides a new CEO, CFO etc.) that a private equity manager will focus on once he invests in a company.

11 CONCLUSIONS

Commercial due diligence is one of the most important parts when private equity investors analyze a company. The company and its business model need to have a lot of specific characteristics in order to represent an attractive investment opportunity for private equity investors. Typically, private equity investors are looking for companies in large and growing markets with high barriers of entry for new competitors. A strong competitive position of the company with a large market share and pricing power towards customers and suppliers is another aspect that investors are looking for. The products or services should have high EBITDA margins in order to generate high cash flows that can be used to repay the debt that was used to finance the transaction. The products and services of the company should be mission critical for customers, such that customers relationships are long-lasting (low customer churn) and revenue is predicable (high recurring revenue). These aspects will be the basis for a successful value creation strategy, whereas value creation happens through EBITDA increase, through multiple arbitrage (selling for higher valuation levels than initially paid for) and through deleveraging, i.e. repaying debt. A capable and experienced top management team is essential to ensure that the value creation strategy is executed successfully. Therefore, private equity investors spend a lot of time and energy to find the perfect executives for every success-critical position within a company, e.g. the CEO, CFO or COO role.

APPENDIX 1: CHECKLIST

Revenue model checklist:
- Revenue stability
- Revenue mix by geography, products (segments) and industry exposure
- Product/service portfolio
- Value proposition of products/services
- Pricing opportunities (e.g. potential price increases)
- Pricing history (discounts, price increases etc.)
- Cross Selling and upselling opportunities
- Contract type (subscription based vs. transaction based)
- Revenue stickiness, i.e. share of recurring revenue

Cost structure checklist:
- Cost structure analysis (Fixed cost versus variable costs)
- Cost cutting opportunities
- Cost (driver) and margin analysis
- Margin sustainability and stability
- Earnings quality
- Working capital management (working capital requirements, working capital cycle, stock keeping units, improvement opportunities)
- Operational leverage analysis (Unit economics, contribution margins, variable cost productivity)
- Benchmark cost structure, earnings margins and cash flow

conversion with competitors as well as industry averages
- Availability of cost efficiencies

Organization checklist:
- Headquarters, satellite offices and manufacturing sites
- Organizational structure
- Financial and operational key performance indicator (KPI) reporting
- Efficiency of corporate processes
- customer relationship management tools (CRM), enterprise resource planning (ERP) tools and financial accounting systems
- State of IT infrastructure (relates also to IT due diligence)
- Intellectual property and patents (related to legal DD)

Market checklist:
- Size of total addressable market (TAM), serviceable available market (SAM) and serviceable obtainable market (SOM)
- End market exposure
- Historical growth rate and expected future growth rates
- Long-term market secular trends/supply and demand trends
- Macro risks and GDP sensitivity (cyclicality)
- Regulatory environment
- Tariff environment

Competition checklist:
- Nature of competition
- Barriers to enter the market
- Level of market fragmentation
- Number of competitors
- Key competitors and their strategic positioning
- (Historic and current) market shares in the total market and in sub-markets (divided by geography, product category etc.)
- Market positioning of company
- Historical and expected future performance compared to key competitors (sales growth, margins, market share etc.)
- Competitive differentiator of company
- USP of products/services

- Reputation and brand recognition of company
- Opportunities for strategic add-on transactions

Customer checklist:

- Customer portfolio (number of customers and trading volume of each customer)
- Duration of relationship with customers and access to key decision maker (especially for largest customers)
- Past success in winning new customers (historic win rate)
- Historic customer churn
- Pipeline of new customers
- Target customer groups
- Customer concentration (Top 10 or Top 20 customers by revenue)
- Financial strength/solvency of customers
- Customer Satisfaction
- Customer pricing power and price sensitivity
- Customer demographics
- Customer/Demand trends
- Customer surveys/reference calls
- Review of customer contracts (related to legal DD)

Supplier checklist:

- Number of suppliers
- Historic relationship with suppliers (annual volume and years of cooperation)
- Dependence of suppliers
- Product/service portfolio of supplier
- Quality of suppliers' products/services
- Pricing power of suppliers
- Supplier reliance and customer service quality
- Availability of alternative suppliers
- Supplier reference checks/calls

Management and other human resources checklist:

- Number of FTEs
- Split of FTEs between different areas of company (e.g. marketing, sales, IT etc.)
- Average age and average tenure of FTEs
- Historic FTE turnover
- Organizational culture
- Quality of FTEs (years of experience, industry knowledge, academic education etc.)
- Lack of FTEs in certain areas of the company (e.g. in sales department)
- Dependent on key executives (e.g. founder, that knows ins and outs of company) or CTO (who has key knowledge regarding IT structure of company)
- Sales team capacity and marketing performance
- Human resource approach and success in winning new FTEs
- IT know-how of FTEs
- Availability and cost of skilled/trained employees on job market
- Possibilities to reduce workforce due to overstaffing in certain areas of the company
- Potential to outsource/digitize labor-intensive tasks
- Dependence of third-party contractors
- Background checks and references calls on management
- Interviews and meetings with top management and other key FTEs
- Founder/Seller rollover
- Management incentives (e.g. sweet equity)
- Existence and strength of labor unions
- History of labor unions and labor strikes

APPENDIX 2: ABBREVIATIONS

CAPEX	capital expenditure
CEO	chief executive officer
CFO	chief financial officer
COO	chief operating officer
CRM	customer relationship management
CTO	chief technology officer
DD	due diligence
EBIT	earnings before interest and tax
EBITDA	earnings before interest, tax, depreciation and amortization
ERP	enterprise resource planning
ESG	environmental, Social and Governance
EV	enterprise value
FTE	full-time employee
KPI	key performance indicator
Mio.	million
PE	private Equity
SaaS	software as a service
SAM	serviceable available market
SOM	serviceable obtainable market
TAM	total addressable market
USD	United States dollar
USP	unique selling proposition

Made in the USA
Las Vegas, NV
22 April 2024

88983592R00024